TRUMP
and the **FUTURE** of
AMERICA

JEREMIAH JOHNSON

Jeremiah Johnson Ministries
1816 Lynncrest Rd.
Lakeland, FL 33801

Cover Design by Esther Eunjoo Jun
Interior Design by Susan Ramundo

To order any of Jeremiah's books or other resources, please visit:
www.jeremiahjohnson.tv

ISBN: 978-1-7107-4625-9
Imprint: Independently published

OTHER BOOKS BY JEREMIAH JOHNSON

I See a New Prophetic Generation
I See a New Apostolic Generation
The Micaiah Company
Cleansing and Igniting the Prophetic
Cleansing and Igniting the Prophetic Study Guide
Trump, 2019 & Beyond
The Power of Consecration
Judgment on the House of God

To receive email updates, read blogs, purchase resources, become a ministry partner, or follow Jeremiah's travel itinerary, please visit www.JeremiahJohnson.tv

DEDICATION

This book is dedicated to my father Joseph Johnson, who gave me my love for history and helped me embrace the call of God on my life from a very early age. Dad, thanks for always taking me to church early with you as a kid and asking me what God revealed in my dreams the night before. You gave a little boy permission to be bold and courageous and believe that God did not write a book and then lose His voice. May the father, husband, and prophetic voice I have become simply be a testimony to your commitment to me as your son. I love you pops!

TABLE OF CONTENTS

FOREWORD

Daniel 9:2-3 says, "In the first year of his reign I, Daniel, understood by the books the number of the years specified by the word of the Lord through Jeremiah the prophet, that He would accomplish seventy years in the desolations of Jerusalem. Then I set my face toward the Lord God to make request by prayer and supplications, with fasting, sackcloth, and ashes."

Prophetic promises carry conditions. When Daniel did the math that showed him that the 70 years of Babylonian captivity were up, Daniel set himself to fast, pray and repent. Why would he do that if the promise of Israel's restoration was guaranteed? That question hits the present danger for many in the prophetic movement who feel entitled to Trump's re-election. But, I do believe his re-election is promised to a people who will pray, fast, repent, and here's the big one: work hard.

Jeremiah Johnson has written down both a warning and guidance. He has faithfully related the dealings of God in his own life. He has courageously shared what he has received from the Holy Spirit about Trump and the future of America. This places him in a very high level of scrutiny. Every prophetic word must be anchored to the Bible. No dream, impression or vision should be accepted without verification—and true prophets yearn for confirmation. Jesus said in John 3:21, "But he who does the truth comes to the light, that his deeds may be clearly seen, that they have been done in God."

In a time when "words from the Lord" are merchandized like palm readings and horoscopes, we need accuracy, purity and clarity. There will be special punishment in this life and in the next for those who willfully pointed the sheep of God in the wrong direction. On the other hand, we must not allow counterfeits to be an excuse to squelch the true gifts.

Why would we reject a road map complete with the locations of the land mines? Why not arm yourself with insights that will not only reduce the danger of the future but allow you to thrive in dark times? Don't be sidelined and victimized by 2020. Rather, read, discern and act in accordance with the Word of God. That is what this book is designed to give you.

—Mario Murillo, International Speaker and Author
of *Critical Mass* and *Vessels of Fire and Glory.*

To follow and subscribe to Mario's ministry, please visit MarioMurillo.org.

INTRODUCTION

We are at a time when the consequences of our electoral decisions and governmental engagement will impact the nations for generations to come. The choices being made now in the high places of our government are having a profound ripple effect throughout the earth. The Church, however, has yet to take full responsibility for our commission at this point in history. We have been called as Kingdom ambassadors to transform our culture and demonstrate viable Kingdom authority—right in the middle of enemy occupation.

The Lord says to my Lord, "Sit at my right hand, until I make your enemies your footstool." The Lord sends forth from Zion Your mighty scepter. Rule in the midst of Your enemies! (Psalms 110:1-2 ESV)

There are demonic strongholds deeply embedded within the man-made political systems on the earth, the Church, the rising "Ecclesia" of God, has been given authority from heaven to shift things through prayer and demonstrate righteous rule on the earth. We have been uniquely set apart to be empowered change agents in our nation by representing a King whose government will never end. Though many believers have awakened to this call, there are many who are yet sitting on the sidelines, either unaware of the battles, too weary to join in the fight, or too apathetic to care.

We have been commanded to pray for our nation and all those in positions of authority (see 1 Tim 2:1-3). It is the prayers from a righteous and holy people that attract heaven and cause our intercession to be powerful and effective. We must win the war in the heavenlies if we are to see transformation on the earth. It is the Ecclesia that has the legitimate spiritual authority to guard, keep, and occupy this nation for the glory of God.

To the one who is victorious and does My will to the end, I will give authority over the nations. (Revelation 2:26 NIV)

For the remnant that is awake and responding to the alarm of the watchmen, our passion is noble, but our numbers are few. The corporate body of Christ has yet to be of "one mind and one spirit" in order to displace the ungodly rulers of the day. We are still divided as to the priorities at hand and unable to agree on a proper diagnosis that can bring a heavenly resolution. It is only when we see beyond the fog of human reasoning and personal opinion that we can rightly discern by the Spirit what is actually taking place and how we must respond. It is only when we agree on the problem that we will know how to pray.

The first step we must take in addressing the squatting spiritual giants in our land is to reveal the supernatural realities in the heavenly realms. It is the prophetic charge to reveal these truths in order to call the Church to prayer and to action. Jeremiah Johnson does that in this book. By sharing the powerful dreams and words he has received from the Lord, he is giving us a specific target. He is revealing the strongholds and principalities at work in high places so that believers can rightly pray and appropriately intervene.

The Lord has given Jeremiah a unique gift of dreams by which the Lord is not only revealing the enemy's schemes but teaching the Church how to respond. Through these dreams and visions, we are being given intercessory intelligence in order to target our prayers with corporate authority.

As a lifelong intercessor and a fellow prophetic voice to the nation, I have had numerous dreams concerning this nation and our president. Being a writer for a national prayer ministry has also connected me with countless other faithful intercessors with similar encounters. Where many prophetic dreams tend to be highly symbolic and prone to subjective interpretation, Jeremiah's dreams are much more pointed. His dreams leave little room for subjective interpretation simply because of the specificity of the details. His dreams provide prophetic clarity and revelations from heaven that are calling the Church to take its place on the wall of prayer as well engage more intentionally in the public square.

One of the consistent roadblocks I have seen in the national prayer movement is the lack of corporate authority needed to displace corporate strongholds. It is one thing to walk in spiritual authority as a believer on our own turf. It is another to walk in corporate authority on behalf of a nation. Not only does this require a unity of heart and mind within the larger body, it requires legitimate authority from its leaders. The Church is still stumbling as we deal with broken pastors, fallen ministers, and counterfeit messengers that have weakened our stand and limited our influence, both in the natural as well as the spiritual. We need to see more church leaders rise up who are free from personal ambition, the fear of man, and an unhealthy need for validation, so that our corporate intercession is recognized by sanctified spiritual authority.

I believe Jeremiah Johnson has been prepared for this time as he has held the bar high in his own life and ministry. His commitment to integrity and passion for purity is refreshing in today's climate of grace-filled sound bites. He is uncompromising in his message and demonstrates a fear of the Lord that is much needed. Thus far, his prophetic revelations have been accurate and served to empower and embolden the body of Christ in this season.

By reading and sharing this book with others, I believe our faith can be strengthened and our intercession stirred to new levels of power and effectiveness. By prayerfully considering these messages from the Lord, we should grow deeper in spiritual discernment as well as receive an impartation for similar revelations in our own prayer closets.

But, be warned. This message is time sensitive. It cannot tarry and it cannot be put on hold. We have a window of opportunity that must be seized now. I urge you to take heed and commit yourself to prayer, not only for this nation, but for the body of Christ. Our legacy depends on it.

—Wanda Alger, Field Correspondent,
Intercessors for America
Author, *Prayer That Sparks National Revival*
and *Moving From Sword to Scepter:*
Ruling through Prayer as the Ecclesia of God

CHAPTER 1

KEEP YOUR EYES OPEN

On January 10, 2019, I self-published the first book in this series: *Trump, 2019, and Beyond.* I never imagined that within thirty days of publication, *Trump, 2019, and Beyond* would become the number one best seller in seven different categories on Amazon. In one year, it sold more copies than my eight other books combined. We have also received confirmation from several reliable sources that the book has made it into the White House and into the hands of many high-ranking government officials who are reading it.

When publishing the dreams and visions contained in *Trump, 2019, and Beyond,* I desired to give the Church a clear prayer agenda and prophetically assist believers in understanding the times and seasons in which we live. After reading the book, Mary Gibson wrote, "*Trump, 2019, and Beyond* is surely present day revelation from God to the nations to wake up! Jeremiah Johnson clearly details what God has revealed concerning Donald Trump and how we can pray. It also is a book of hope and encourages us to put

God first in all things."[1] Another reader, Ronda Nunez, commented, "Jeremiah's dreams and visions are a great source of wisdom to me as an intercessor. Upon reading this book, my heart was gripped with deep repentance to pray and fight for our nation and our president."[2]

A SPECIAL VISIT

As the prophetic dreams and visions contained in *Trump, 2019, and Beyond* began to circle the globe and invitations to television and radio shows poured in, a particular gentleman contacted me, requesting a special meeting. After I agreed to meet with him, he introduced himself as a professor at a well-known university who had been documenting every prophecy concerning Donald Trump in the last five to ten years. He had even written an impressive book chronicling all the prophecies in alphabetical order according to their author's last name.

After browsing the book for several minutes, I looked at him. "You have recorded hundreds of saints and well-known leaders in this book who have given prophecies about Donald Trump," I said. "Out of all of them, why did you want to meet with me?"

---

1. Mary Gibson, Review, amazon.com, 16 January 2019, https://www.amazon.com/Trump-2019-Beyond-Jeremiah-Johnson-ebook/dp/B07MQ86QPQ.
2. Ronda Nunez, Review, amazon.com, 19 January 2019, https://www.amazon.com/Trump-2019-Beyond-Jeremiah-Johnson-ebook/dp/B07MQ86QPQ.

"Because," he replied, "you are the only one I have found to give both positive and warning prophecies concerning Donald Trump."

Then he asked, "So what is God showing you about Trump and the future of America now?"

From what I shared with him then and the dreams and visions God has given me over the months since, this book was birthed!

TWO AREAS OF CONCERN

I am compelled by the Holy Spirit to point out two areas of specific concern regarding Donald Trump and the future of America that were referenced in the first book and currently burden me. These two issues must be kept in prayer as you read this sequel.

In Chapter 4 of *Trump, 2019, and Beyond*, I shared a prophetic dream in which I saw Donald Trump crawling around on the White House lawn, eating grass and acting like an animal.[3] Immediately I cried out to the Lord in the dream and asked, "God, shall Donald Trump become like Nebuchadnezzar?" God spoke back to me in the dream and said, "Donald Trump is in great danger of becoming

---

3. Jeremiah Johnson, *Trump, 2019, and Beyond*, Chapter 4, "The Nebuchadnezzar Warning," p. 43.

like Nebuchadnezzar in the years ahead. He will have great success but the church must pray for humility."

Later, on August 21, 2019, Donald Trump posted a tweet thanking Wayne Allyn Root for his "very nice words."[4] What had Root said that elicited this acknowledgement from the President?

"President Trump is the greatest President for Jews and for Israel in the history of the world, not just for America," Root said. "The Jewish people love him like he's the king of Israel. They love him like he is the second coming of God."[5]

While the President himself was not the author of these statements, he did take notice of them, drawing them to public attention through his tweet. That alone is alarming, but for Donald Trump to thank Root for making highly questionable—bordering on blasphemous—comments, asserting that the American president is like "the king of Israel" and the "second coming of God," should concern earnest Jews and Christians alike. Could this be a prophetic sign to the intercessors and watchmen, directing us to once again make the pride and arrogance of President Donald Trump a focus of our prayers?

---

4. President Donald Trump, 21 August 2019, 4:34 am, https://twitter.com/real donaldtrump/status/1164138795475881986?lang=en.

5. Wayne Allyn Root, "Trump Cites Newsmax, Wayne Root on Jews," Newsmax .com, 21 August 2019, https://www.newsmax.com/newsfront/trump-wayne -allyn-root-newsmax-tv-jews/2019/08/21/id/929371/.

And is God orchestrating events in our nation that are meant to humble Trump and reveal what is in his heart?

Secondly, in Chapter 5 of *Trump, 2019, and Beyond*, I shared that God had revealed to me that Sarah Huckabee, Nikki Haley, and Mike Pence were specifically carrying an anointing to give Donald Trump sound counsel at strategic moments of his presidency.

"If Sarah Huckabee, Mike Pence, and Nikki Haley resign, are fired, or there is tension and disagreement with Trump," I wrote, "I believe it could be an indicator that trouble is ahead."[6]

As we enter into 2020, Sarah Huckabee and Nikki Haley have indeed both resigned. If God was truly speaking when I wrote the last book in 2018, the intercessors, saints, and watchmen must keep Donald Trump in prayer like never before. God is clearly revealing a root of pride and arrogance in him that typically manifests as fear and anger online and in private circles. Could God also be orchestrating national and personal events in the life of Donald Trump that are primarily intended to break his will and teach him how to trust and depend, like Nebuchadnezzar, on God?

---

6. Jeremiah Johnson, *Trump, 2019, and Beyond*, Chapter 5, "The Daniel Company," p. 49.

We must pray for an increase in the strategic placement of godly men and women around Donald Trump who will faithfully deliver the word of the Lord to him as he seeks to guide our nation in the days ahead.

As you read the prophetic dreams, visions, and personal commentary in the pages ahead, be sure to make a clear prayer agenda and ask God how you also might get involved in the political race in 2020. Read this book in one setting if you must, but then go back and invite the Holy Spirit to reveal the heights and depths of His great and mighty plans that He has for the United States of America. If the worst of times are ahead of us, so are the best!

CHAPTER 1 Prayer Points

- Pray for President Trump to walk humbly.
- Pray Proverbs 16:7, Psalm 25:9, Micah 6:8, Colossians 3:12-13, and James 4:10 over him.
- Pray for godly counsel to be released to President Trump and received by him.
- Pray Proverbs 19:20-21 over him.

CHAPTER 2

A SHOCKING VISIT TO THE WHITE HOUSE

In a prophetic dream in early February of 2019, I arrived at the White House in a white limousine. Security guards met me and immediately escorted me to the President's office. When I knocked on the door, it automatically opened and I walked in to find Donald Trump staring into an oval mirror.

It was not the President's reflection looking back at him. To my shock, in the mirror Abraham Lincoln steadily returned Donald Trump's gaze, eye to eye, face to face.

Clearly caught off guard, the President hurriedly acknowledged my presence and asked me to take a chair in front of his desk. He sat across from me, and we chit-chatted for a while about current events in America and his personal life and family.

When the conversation reached a certain point, I leaned over to him and said, "Mr. President, I have been sent here to reveal to you the three main principalities that are opposing you in this nation. You must be aware of their presence and their identities if you are to understand how to navigate the days ahead."

At that moment, I noticed a large window directly behind him, covered by a curtain. "Sir," I asked, "what is behind that window?"

The President seemed unconcerned. "The White House lawn," he said.

I leapt from my chair and ripped the curtain back from the window. There before us on the White House lawn stood three gigantic principalities, each about forty feet tall each. They stood one next to the other in a line, full of life.

I pointed at the first being and said to the President, "The first principality you are dealing with in the United States is the principality of racism. It is an ancient evil in this country that will attempt to entice you into its jaws again and again. It has dwelled on these grounds for many, many years, and you must eradicate it if war is to be avoided in the coming days."

As I talked, Donald Trump stood at attention like a military officer, following my words intently but silent.

I pointed to the next principality, shaped like a woman with large horns on her head.

"This is the principality of 'radical feminism'," I told him. "It will seek to pierce your heart and plunge a dagger into it. She will stalk you in the days ahead and she will overcome you if you tolerate her. You must continue to confront her and take your stand."

Finally I pointed to the third principality.

"This is the principality called Molech," I explained to the President in the dream. "It feeds off the shedding of innocent blood in this nation. You must understand that all three of these principalities are interconnected. You have been chosen and raised up for such a time as this so that these three monsters might be defeated and the future of this country restored to the people of the United States of America."

Then Donald Trump asked if I would pray for him. After doing so, I was escorted out of the White House and back to the white limousine.

Then I woke up.

CHAPTER 2   Prayer Points

- Pray for President Trump to be strengthened in his inner man with power through the Spirit, to discern good and evil, to be strong in the Lord, and to fulfill his calling.
- Pray Ephesians 3:16.
- Pray Ephesians 6:10-17.

CHAPTER 3

THE MAN IN THE MIRROR

One would expect, on waking from such a dream, that I would immediately be drawn into intercession and prayer concerning the three principalities opposing Donald Trump and threatening the future of the United States of America. However, when I first awoke, I was most shaken and burdened by the face of that famous man that I saw in the mirror when I first walked into the President's office.

I was so shocked to see the face of Abraham Lincoln staring back at Donald Trump in that mirror. What could this portend? What was God trying to show me?

What possible connection could there be between Donald Trump and Abraham Lincoln?

I waited and sat in prayer over this for many months. I sensed I was being invited by the Spirit of God to study the faith of America's founding fathers. The Lord impressed upon me that only then could I understand how Donald Trump was being strategically and divinely placed in a time of crisis in American history, just as his predecessor

Abraham Lincoln had been. More importantly, like Lincoln, how Trump responds to this crisis will determine the fate of future generations of Americans.

THE SHALLOW FAITH
OF THE FOUNDING FATHERS

The founding fathers were politicians and philosophers, churchmen and doubters. They were well acquainted with history, theology, business, and soldiering. They explored religious ideas, but only a few of them could be considered bold witnesses of the Christian faith.

In fact, Thomas Jefferson edited the gospels[7], and Benjamin Franklin rephrased and rearranged the Book of Common Prayer.[8] Later both would question the divinity of Jesus Christ.[9] The religious ideas of many of the founding fathers were influenced by deism. Jefferson and Franklin believed that Jesus of Nazareth was a great moral teacher—perhaps the greatest in all of human history—but, each eventually concluded, he could not be the Son

---

7. Owen Edwards, "How Thomas Jefferson Created His Own Bible," *Smithsonian Magazine*, January 2012, https://www.smithsonianmag.com/arts-culture/how-thomas-jefferson-created-his-own-bible-5659505/.

8. Barbara B. Oberg and Harry S. Stout, eds., *Benjamin Franklin, Jonathan Edwards, and the Representation of American Culture*, (New York, Oxford University Press, 1993), 38.

9. Lehrman Institute, "The Founders' Faith," lehrmaninstitute.org, 29 November 2019, https://lehrmaninstitute.org/history/the-founders-faith.html#ben.

of God. They also believed the doctrine of the Trinity was a corrupt invention of the institutional church.[10]

John Adams considered pursuing a call of ministry on his life, but chose to study law instead and lived his life as a Unitarian.[11]

Many of the founders grew up and grew old in religious households. While religion has always been woven into American politics, to say that America was founded as a "Christian nation" could be very misleading.

Did the founding fathers have a sense of inner conscience that led them to believe that God was the Creator of all things and worked His will into their lives and the nation in some form?

Absolutely.

But to paint a picture or vision of history where our founding fathers were men of conviction concerning the inerrancy of Scripture, the divinity of Christ, and the reality of heaven and hell is a grave mistake.

Perhaps an even more alarming question is this: do we now in the twenty-first century require presidents—men like Donald Trump—to adhere to higher standards of faith and practice than those of their predecessors? Rather than claim that America was founded as a "Christian nation," it would be more accurate to say that America was

10. Ibid.
11. Ibid.

founded by men guided by Christian principles, however sincere or shallow their personal faith in Jesus Christ might have been.

For example, in a treaty with the Muslim nation of Tripoli initiated by George Washington in 1797, John Adams and the Senate declared that "the government of the United States is not in any sense founded on the Christian Religion…"[12] How shocking!

WHY CHRISTIANS REFUSE TO VOTE FOR DONALD TRUMP

As I began to evaluate the shallow faith of the founding fathers, I was deeply troubled in my spirit. Their lack of personal conviction was not the source of this disturbance. Rather, it was the discrepancy between the standard set by our earliest presidents and the standard applied by the twenty-first century church in voting for current presidents.

I have been berated on multiple occasions both publicly and privately for suggesting that Christians could vote for Donald Trump. "There is no way that man is a Christian!" is the typical response of the offended believer.

---

12. Morton Borden, *Jews, Turks, and Infidels*, (Chapel Hill, University of North Carolina Press, 1984), 76–79.

Would they have voted for George Washington? Thomas Jefferson? John Adams?

Benjamin Franklin denied the divinity of Christ and George Washington initiated a treaty that claimed America is not a Christian nation. Evangelicals and Pentecostals alike would be in an uproar if these men were alive today and running for the highest office in the land.

It is true that, in 1892, a unanimous Supreme Court stated that "We find everywhere a clear recognition of the same truth… this is a Christian nation."[13] However, America was found to be a "Christian nation" in the sense that it was a nation populated by people who identified themselves as Christians

ABRAHAM LINCOLN AND DONALD TRUMP

I was awakened by the Spirit of God to this truth: many Christians did not and will not vote for Donald Trump because they have an inaccurate view of the faith of his predecessors and a misleading definition of America as a "Christian nation." Now I felt impressed by the Spirit to examine the life and faith of Abraham Lincoln. What I discovered was very interesting.

---

13. *Holy Trinity Church v. United States*, 143 U.S. 457, 471 (1892). https://cdn.loc .gov/service/ll/usrep/usrep143/usrep143457/usrep143457.pdf.

Lincoln was charged with being a "scoffer of religion" when he ran for the House of Representatives from Illinois because he belonged to no church.[14] During the campaign, Lincoln attended a service where his opponent in the race, Reverend Peter Cartwright, delivered the sermon. Cartwright was a Methodist evangelist.

At a dramatic moment in his preaching, Cartwright said, "All who do not wish to go to hell will stand."

Only Lincoln remained seated.

"May I inquire of you, Mr. Lincoln," the minister asked, "where you are going?"

"I am going to Congress," replied the unruffled Lincoln.[15]

Like Lincoln, the faith of Donald Trump has been questioned repeatedly by multitudes of Christians across the United States. Whether offended by his tweets or critical of his apparent lack of "depth" as a believer in Jesus Christ, we hold Donald Trump to higher standards for a Christian president than those expected of past presidents like Abraham Lincoln.

Despite Lincoln's tongue-in-cheek reply to his opponent Peter Cartwright, he repeatedly claimed that his

---

14. William J. Wolf, *The Almost Chosen People: A Study of the Religion of Abraham Lincoln*, (New York, Doubleday, 1959).
15. Ibid, 69.

"constant anxiety and prayer is that I and this nation should be on the Lord's side."[16]

It is absolutely true that a president's private faith will inevitably inform his public life in office.

THE CIVIL WAR

Abraham Lincoln had been president for a little more than a month when the Civil War erupted. On March 4, 1861, in his inaugural address, Lincoln begged the nation for forbearance, asking for "intelligence, patriotism, Christianity, and firm reliance on Him, who has never yet forsaken this favored land."[17] Later on March 30, 1863, President Lincoln issued a Proclamation for a Day of Fasting, Humiliation, and Prayer concerning the issue of slavery in the United States.[18]

As we seek to understand how the Holy Spirit might possibly be connecting Donald Trump with Abraham Lincoln, it is important to note how Lincoln connects his statements about slavery with God. Concerning slavery and the Civil War, Lincoln vowed, "Fondly do we hope—fervently do we pray—that this mighty scourge of war may speedily pass away."

---

16. Ibid, 128.
17. Abraham Lincoln, *Abraham Lincoln: Speeches and Writings Volume 2: 1859–1865*, (New York, Library of America, 1989), 213–214.
18. Ibid, 264.

But he qualified this statement as follows: "Yet, if God wills that it continue, until all the wealth piled by the bond-man's two hundred and fifty years of unrequited toil shall be sunk, and until every drop of blood drawn with the lash, shall be paid by another drawn with the sword, as we said three thousand years ago, so still it must be said: 'The judgments of the Lord are true and righteous altogether.'"[19]

In this stunning speech, Abraham Lincoln clearly identifies the Civil War as God's judgment on the United States of America because of slavery. In sharp contrast to the presidents before him, Lincoln seemed to interpret the troubles of his times in explicitly Christian fashion.

On Wednesday, February 10, 1864, a group of ministers came together to ask the President and Congress to support the passage of the following amended Preamble to the Constitution of the United States of America:

"We, the people of the United States, humbly acknowledging Almighty God as the source of all authority and power in civil government, the Lord Jesus Christ, as the Ruler among the nations, and His revealed will as of supreme authority, in order to constitute a Christian government, and in order to form a more perfect union…"[20]

---

19. Ibid, 686–687.
20. Gaines M. Foster, *Moral Reconstruction: Christian Lobbyists and the Federal Legislation of Morality, 1865–1920*, (Chapel Hill, University of North Carolina Press, 2002), 2.

THE GOOD FRIDAY ASSASSINATION

Lincoln replied that he would examine their paper in the days ahead, but on Good Friday, April 14, 1865, he was assassinated at the time of Passover, in the closing weeks of war. One thing remains certain: America emerged from the gloom of the Civil War stronger, freer, and more firmly unified because of Abraham Lincoln's faith in and discernment of God's ways.

After researching and discovering the shallow faith of the founding fathers, and then being shown that Abraham Lincoln possessed a sincere desire personally and on behalf of the nation to seek the God of the Bible, I found myself in heavy intercession and prayer. One question burned in my heart: "God, if you elevated Abraham Lincoln at a strategic time in American history (the Civil War) because his calling for prayer and fasting and recognizing God's judgments would determine the future of the nation, why have you elevated Donald Trump now and what response do You desire from him to determine the future of this nation?"

God's reply was simple.

He raised up Abraham Lincoln, an imperfect man of religious faith, during the Civil War to issue the Emancipation Proclamation in an attempt to free the slaves and call for a National Day of Prayer, Humiliation, and Fasting. Likewise, He has raised up Donald Trump, an imperfect man of religious faith, during the greatest holocaust the world has ever witnessed; the shedding of over sixty million babies' blood.

If Abraham Lincoln recognized the 600,000 casualties of the Civil War as the judgment of God on a nation because of slavery, what awaits the United States over the bloodshed of more than 60 million babies?

Should American Christians be fervently praying, fasting, and crying out for the ending of *Roe v. Wade*, or should the Church stay out of politics and encourage believers to avoid voting for Donald Trump because "he doesn't act very Christian"?

CHAPTER 3   Prayer Points

- Pray for President Trump to have ears to hear what the Spirit is saying, to have lips that speak divine decisions, and to have a mind that does not err in judgment.
- Pray for President Trump to be anointed to steer America in a Christian direction.
- Pray for believers to seek God first about who to vote for in elections.
- Pray Revelation 2:29 and Proverbs 16:10.

CHAPTER 4

THE NEXT CIVIL WAR

Ever since I was a child, Christian leaders and preachers alike have urged the Church to stay out of politics. Typically I was told that God is sovereign and all we can do to effect change is pray.

Now as I look back, I wonder, "What has that position achieved in the Church and the nation, and where did that idea come from in the first place?"

JERRY FALWELL WRESTLES WITH GOD

In the 1960's when civil rights were an issue in America, men like Jerry Falwell, founder of Liberty University, preached against ministers getting involved in politics. In his memoir, Falwell quoted himself telling a national convention of clergy that "Our role as pastors and Christian leaders is to attend to the spiritual needs of our people. Serving the church and letting government take care of itself has been my lifelong policy and the policy of my Christian friends and family."[21]

On Tuesday, January 23, 1973, all of that changed for Jerry Falwell.

Reading of the Supreme Court's decision in *Roe v. Wade* in the news, Falwell was "consumed with growing horror and disbelief." As his coffee cooled, he recalled: "I sat there staring at the *Roe v. Wade* story, growing more and more fearful of the consequences of the Supreme Court's act and wondering why so few voices had been raised up against it."[22]

Falwell found himself weighing the personal and professional consequences of plunging into politics to fight abortion. There would be a cost for repudiating his former position of political neutrality. Was he willing to pay it?

His conscience would not allow him to take any other course of action. Eventually Falwell became a central figure among conservative Christian leaders who sought to counter the governmental influence of liberals, secularists, and gay activists.

THE DILEMMA OF BILLY GRAHAM

Billy Graham was one of the most famous and successful evangelists who ever lived. A friend and visitor to the White

---

21. Jerry Falwell, *Strength for the Journey*, (New York, Simon & Schuster, 1987), 334–335.
22. Ibid, 336.

House of several American presidents, Graham tried to have it both ways, dabbling in politics while attempting to remain outside the partisan fray. Things began to heat up for Graham, however, when John F. Kennedy ran against Richard Nixon.

Graham publicly supported Kennedy's candidacy. "Even now," he wrote, "we are wrestling with the forces of anti-Christ on a worldwide scale… We Americans need to decide this election, as it were, on our knees."[23]

What stunning words to the Christian world shared by the world's foremost evangelist during the Kennedy/Nixon election: *"We Americans need to decide this election, as it were, on our knees* [emphasis added]."

What would America in the twenty-first century look like if Christian leaders told church members from pulpits that it was our time to decide elections in the United States and we better do it on our knees praying?

In stark contrast, the *Christian Post* reported just days after the 2016 election that 97 million eligible voters did not cast their vote for a president. I wonder how many of those were Christians who refused to vote because they were taught that the Church does not get involved in politics.

And how many, I wonder, refused to vote for Donald Trump because he was not "Christian enough," totally

---

23. Billy Graham, "We are Electing a President of the World," *Life*, November 7, 1960.

ignoring the shallow faith of Abraham Lincoln and the founding fathers?

THE TIDE IS TURNING

While God has used men like Jerry Falwell and Billy Graham to encourage the Church to get involved in politics and influence elections, from His perspective, perhaps the greatest crisis that has ever threatened the future of the United States of America is abortion: the shedding of more than sixty million babies' blood on U.S. soil. If God lifted up Abraham Lincoln to issue an Emancipation Proclamation attempting to free slaves and re-direct America's future, guiding her through a Civil War, can we believe that He has called Donald Trump to issue another Emancipation Proclamation, confronting abortion in America?

PLEASE TAKE NOTE

It's important to note *Roe v. Wade* does not need to be overturned to end abortion any more than the *Dred Scott* decision needed to be overturned to end slavery. Because the *Roe* decision is both immoral and an act of usurpation, and because abortion is immoral and unconstitutional, it does not need to be overturned because it is not binding. As our first Supreme Court Chief Justice John

Jay said, "Any law repugnant to the Constitution is void." *Roe v. Wade* needs to be defied. Ignored. Just like Ohio and Wisconsin ignored the *Dred Scott* decision and defied Congress' Federal Fugitive Slave Act. States need to ban abortion and interpose between the offending federal power and the innocent they are oath-bound and legally bound to protect.

It's time to pray that another U.S. president will discern the just judgments of God on our nation because of the child sacrifices we have offered to the principality of Molech.

To Donald Trump's credit, on August 19, 2019, Planned Parenthood announced its official withdrawal from the Title X program, costing it $60 million in taxpayer funds, "because it refuses to follow a new Trump administration rule that requires it to segment out its abortion business from legitimate health care if it wants federal funding under the program."[24]

I believe one of the primary reasons why God has elevated Donald Trump in American politics is to end this shedding of innocent blood. Regardless of what our opinions may be, this issue is central in the sight of God, who identifies Himself as "the father of the fatherless and the

---

24. Steven Ertelt, "Trump De-funds Planned Parenthood, Abortion Biz Loses $60 Million in Taxpayer Dollars," lifenews.com, 19 August 2019, https://www.lifenews.com/2019/08/19/trump-defunds-planned-parenthood-abortion-biz-will-lose-60-million-in-taxpayer-dollars/.

protector of widows" (Psalm 68:5). We are in the middle of another type of Civil War and many do not recognize what is at stake. The Church should be repenting on a massive scale and peacefully acting to shut down all known abortion clinics. Believers should seek to adopt unwanted children and support those who are choosing life in this hour.

As we head into the 2020 elections, God has even more to say about this burning issue!

PLEASE CONSIDER THIS

For Donald Trump's entire life, he supported abortion, Planned Parenthood, and even financially gave to the Clinton's campaign. He only declared he was pro-life when he ran for the Republican ticket, and words mean little when actions contradict. We must continue to pray that he would be strong in his stance toward abortion and follow through on his promises to choose pro-life Supreme Court Justices.

CHAPTER 4   Prayer Points

- Pray for the Body of Christ to seek God in repentance.
- Pray for those in authority.
- Pray for God's people to be elected to leadership.
- Lift the fear of politics off the Church.
- Cry out for mercy for America.
- Pray 2 Chronicles 7:14, 1 Timothy 2:1-4, and James 2:13.

CHAPTER 5

A SERIOUS NINEVEH WARNING

Early in 2019, I was taken up in a prophetic dream to an elevated position over the United States from where I saw the word "Nineveh" scrawled across the landscape of the nation. I then was immediately taken into a large courtroom filled with all sorts of angelic beings. Many of these creatures had beautifully colored wings while others had the features of humans, only taller in appearance.

Then the slam of a gavel echoed across the courtroom and all attention shifted to the case currently being tried.

THE UNITED STATES AND NINEVEH

A man in a suit quickly walked into the courtroom carrying a brief case. The words "The Antichrist Spirit" were engraved on the briefcase. The man approached the judge and handed him a paper on which was clearly written, "ABORTION."

The angelic beings in the courtroom seemed to fill with wonder and curiosity. I felt that they were waiting for the judge to make a ruling on the case so that they could know their assignments.

In the dream, the judge began to speak out loud. "The destiny of the United States in hanging in the balance as in the days of Nineveh," he declared. "I once pronounced judgment on Nineveh, and so I now pronounce judgment on the United States of America because they have tolerated the murder of My innocent ones for too long."

The judge continued:

However, I am sending my prophets in the likeness of Jonah from within and without. Yes, I am sending Jonahs from foreign nations that will confront the Antichrist spirit in the United States. Yes, I am also releasing My Jonahs from within the United States who will contend against the Antichrist spirit. Did Nineveh not repent from her wickedness and My hand of judgment relent? Can the United States not repent from her wickedness and My hand of judgment relent concerning this issue of abortion? You must understand that there are many watchmen in the United States whom I have called to take a stand for life, and they have run from it just like Jonah. For this time and in these days, I shall call upon them once more!

LOU ENGLE AND THE
GRAY/WHITE HAIRS

Immediately, the dream shifted to a morgue where I found myself inside a room, waiting for a body to be removed from a bag. When the body was wheeled out before me on a cart and the bag unzipped, I beheld the body of Lou Engle. While he had a very long white beard, in other ways he had the appearance of a physically-fit young man.

I wept in the dream and shouted, "Lou, we need you! The womb of this nation needs you! The intercessors and the prophets need you! Judgment has been decreed upon the land as in the days of Nineveh, but the word of the Lord is that the judgment can be overturned! We must cry out for repentance and mercy in these days!"

Suddenly, one of the angelic beings from the courtroom appeared with a gigantic golden key. The angel plunged the key directly into Lou Engle's heart, and a bolt of lightning hit the room. Lou jumped off the table with a staff in his hands.

He looked at me in the dream and said, "Jeremiah, I once as a young man called the Nazirites forth in this nation, but now as an older man, I will call forth the grandparents in this nation to fight for life!"

Instantly in the dream I felt a witness in the spirit realm. Grandparents in the United States must champion this issue of abortion in their last days! Those in their 50s,

60s, 70s and 80s are carrying specific authority over the principality of Molech.

Lou continued, "I once called upon the long-hairs (Nazirites but now I will call upon the white- and gray-hairs" (grandparents/Baby Boomers).

FIGHTING FOR LIFE IN THE BLACK COMMUNITY

The setting of the dream shifted yet again and I found myself in a sea of people in Washington, D.C. Millions of Christians had gathered on the Mall in front of the Capitol to fight for life.

Lou took the stage with Will and Dehavilland Ford (African-American leaders), and they made a decree to everyone present in the nation.

"Beyond political parties and racial affiliations," Will Ford declared, "we will stand together for life in these days."

Immediately God said to me in the dream, "The issue of abortion will divide African-Americans in the days ahead. Some will refuse to hear what I am saying, while others will be given a justice mandate as never before."

One last time, the dream shifted. My attention was drawn to a newspaper article highlighting an African-American-looking woman. In the years ahead, she would be raised up in politics and force the black community to choose between life in the womb or political party affiliation and race.

I heard God say, "You have been warned, America. What will you do with the judgment of Nineveh upon your nation? Will you fight for life and see mercy fall upon you, or will you remain silent and watch as great destruction and economic collapse fall upon your land?"

Again, I woke up.

CONFRONTING
PLANNED PARENTHOOD

One cannot say, "Black lives matter," and then turn around and support abortion.

Those who know the true history behind Planned Parenthood know that the sole purpose of the project was to destroy the black community. (For example, consider Planned Parenthood's "Negro Project."[25]) To support Planned Parenthood means to support the extermination of black and brown people. Here are some facts.

Margaret Sanger, the founder of Planned Parenthood, is usually described as a "birth control pioneer." Little do people know she met with members of the Klan, advocated eugenics, and supported the use of sterilization to

---

25. Margaret Sanger, "Letter from Margaret Sanger to Dr. C. J. Gamble, 10 December 1939, *Smith Libraries Exhibits*, 29 November 2019, https://libex.smith.edu/omeka/files/original/d6358bc3053c93183295bf2df1c0c931.pdf.

rid the planet of the "unfit" (including black people).[26] As part of her life's work, she advocated for the extermination of African-Americans.[27]

Sanger's original goal for Planned Parenthood was to eliminate black babies before they came into the world. Much of the controversy surrounding her stems from a 1939 letter in which Sanger outlined her plan to reach out to black leaders—specifically ministers—to help dispel community suspicions about the family planning clinics she was opening in the South. Sanger hid behind the guise of "I want to empower women to make their own reproductive choices."

What motivated her was a desire to eliminate what she perceived as inferior human beings.

"We do not want word to go out that we want to exterminate the Negro population," Sanger wrote in a letter to Dr. Clarence Gamble on Dec., 10, 1939.[28]

26. America Needs a Code for Babies," March 27, 1934, Margaret Sanger Papers, Library of Congress, 128:0312B, https://www.nyu.edu/projects/sanger/webedition/app/documents/show.php?sangerDoc=101807.xml. See also Margaret Sanger, "A Plan for Peace," *Birth Control Review*, April 1932, 107–108, and Margaret Sanger, *Woman and the New Race*, (New York, Brentano's, 1920) to appreciate the context of Sanger's use of the term "unfit" and her advocacy of mandatory sterilization. Note especially in this latter work Sanger's distinction between "pure white" races, including the white immigrants from the "Old World" who bring the possibilities of introducing their "rich… traditions of courage, of art, music, letters, science, and philosophy" (p. 36) and those "Negros, Indians, Chinese, and other colored people" (p. 31) who do not come from these "rich" traditions, and who, in the case of the 29 percent illiterate population of the South, are "of course, …Negros" (p. 38).

27. Margaret Sanger, "Letter from Margaret Sanger to Dr. C. J. Gamble, 10 December 1939, *Smith Libraries Exhibits*, 29 November 2019, https://libex.smith.edu/omeka/files/original/d6358bc3053c93183295bf2df1c0c931.pdf.

28. Ibid.

The "unfit," she suggested, should be sent to "farm lands and homesteads" where "they would be taught to work under competent instructors for the period of their entire lives."[29]

Sanger also advocated for a proposal called the "American Baby Code."

"The results desired are obviously selective births," she wrote. The code would "protect society against the propagation and increase of the unfit"[30] and population control would bring about the "materials of a new race."[31]

"If we are to develop in America a new race with a racial soul, we must keep the birth rate within the scope of our ability to understand as well as to educate," Sanger had insisted in an earlier paper. "We must not encourage reproduction beyond *our* capacity to assimilate *our* [white people] numbers so as to make the coming generation into such physically fit, mentally capable, socially alert individuals as are the ideal of a democracy."[32]

Supporting the abortion agenda of Planned Parenthood is supporting the principality of racism: the extermination of black and brown people. As a Christian, to vote for

---

29. Margaret Sanger, "A Plan for Peace," *Birth Control Review*, April 1932, 107–108.

30. America Needs a Code for Babies," March 27, 1934, Margaret Sanger Papers, Library of Congress, 128:0312B, https://www.nyu.edu/projects/sanger/web edition/app/documents/show.php?sangerDoc=101807.xml.

31. Margaret Sanger, *Woman and the New Race*, (New York, Brentano's, 1920), 14.

32. Ibid.

politicians who support abortion makes one an accomplice of racism.

THE RISE OF PROPHETIC ACTIVISTS

The Church stands in the middle of the greatest fight for life the world has ever known. The price of resisting the principality of racism in Abraham Lincoln's day was 600,000 soldiers. In Donald Trump's day, the price of resisting the principality of Molech is 60 million innocent babies. Can the Church with one voice kneel in repentance and ask God to forgive our wickedness and heal our land? Can believers in Jesus Christ commit to never vote for a political candidate again that supports abortion?

The Scriptures are clear in Jeremiah 19 as God explains why the people of Judah were about to go into exile: They worshipped idols and they "filled this place (speaking of Jerusalem) with the blood of the innocent. They have built the high places of Baal to burn their children in the fire as offerings to Baal" (Jeremiah 19:4-5).

America stands on the brink of exile because of the Church's passivity about abortion, and in some quarters, support for abortion. We have fed Molech too long in this nation and the time has come to repent and stop the madness. When will preacher and saint alike arise and say enough is enough?

Christian philosopher Francis Schaeffer reportedly put it this way: "Every abortion clinic should have a sign in front of it say, 'Open by Permission of the Church.'"[33]

I see God using the gray/white-hairs in America to turn the tide and place us back on the path of righteousness. The 2020 elections will be defined by an older remnant in America who understands the judgments of God and the consequences for our country for the shedding of innocent blood.

Now is the time to rise and shine. There is yet time to repent!

33. Samuel A. Morris, "Open by Permission of the Church?," samuelamorrisblogspot .com, 26 August 2015, http://samuelamorris.blogspot.com/2015/08/open-by -permission-of-church.html.

CHAPTER 5   Prayer Points

- Pray for the sleeping church to awaken to the perilous times in which we are living.
- Ask the Lord for His kindness to lead us to repentance.
- Pray for church leaders to have utterance with boldness concerning abortion, radical feminism, and racism.
- Pray Romans 2:4 and Ephesians 6:19.
- Pray and do 2 Chronicles 7:14.
- Pray for light and truth to be released over our nation.
- Pray for the Church to take a stand for life.

CHAPTER 6

THE RISE OF RADICAL FEMINISM

One of the three principalities that I pointed out to Donald Trump in my dream that he was facing in America is the principality of "radical feminism." As President Trump delivered the State of the Union address on February 5, 2019, seated in the audience before him were hundreds of women who chose to wear "white coats" to represent freedom for women's rights in America. As the President gave positive updates on the nation and reported key decisions regarding the ending of late term-abortion, this group of women wearing white coats sat like statues, refusing to participate in the applause.

This principality on the White House lawn was shaped like a woman with large horns on her head. This principality is the spirit of radical feminism. It attended his State of the Union speech not to listen and consider but as an act of war.

EXPOSING THE RADICAL
FEMINIST SPIRIT

We must understand that the radical feminist spirit will never embrace life in the womb because it is a spirit of independence from and rebellion toward God. The Bible tells us that God is not just the source of life; He is Life Itself (John 1:4, 14:6). In God's hand is the life of every created being, (Job 12:10). To separate from God is to separate from life, and to separate from life is to separate from God. The promotion of abortion is the natural consequence of denying the presence of life in the womb. The radical feminist spirit cannot acknowledge life in the womb without undermining its real agenda.

The only time the radical feminist spirit can prevail is when it is given attention and applause. Like a two-year-old throwing a tantrum to get its own way, the radical feminist spirit is a master emotional and physical controller and manipulator. This principality manifests loudest under God-given authority.

"With their own hands the pitiful women have boiled their own children," grieves Jeremiah in Lamentations 4:10 of the women under God's judgement in Judah.

How true this rings today in America! In my dream-visit with Donald Trump, the three ruling principalities facing him on the lawn of the White House—racism, radical feminism, and abortion—are all intertwined. Radical feminism has legislated the slaughter of millions of babies and specifically targets the African American community. When we understand the underlying attitude toward African Americans and the belief system of the founder of Planned Parenthood, Margaret Sanger, the connection between all three of these principalities becomes clearer.

In his book *Jezebel's War with America*, Dr. Michael Brown warns the Church that "Jezebel is aggressive. She is obsessed. She is determined. 'I must have my right to abort!' Abortion is considered a matter of reproductive justice by Jezebel."[34] Could another name for the spirit of radical feminism be the spirit of Jezebel? Are speaker of the house Nancy Pelosi and New York congresswoman Alexandria Ocasio-Cortez simply manifestations of the radical feminist principality seeking the destruction of a "Christian nation"?

"How close is our nation to experiencing the fury of God's wrath?" ponders Brown. "To ignore that question is to bury our heads in the sand. America is teetering even closer to collapse than ever before. Abortion was the number one cause of death worldwide in 2018, with more than 41 million children killed before birth."[35]

34. Michael Brown, *Jezebel's War with America*, (FrontLine, 2019), 74.
35. Ibid, 76–77.

CHAPTER 6   Prayer Points

- Pray for God to rescue women from the deception of feminism.
- Pray that God would open our eyes to truth.
- Pray that God would expose the rebellion, the racism, and the death hiding in this movement.
- Pray that God would deliver us from evil.

CHAPTER 7

THE ENTERTAINMENT MOUNTAIN REVIVAL

Meet Donald Trump, Justin Bieber, and Kanye West; three men anointed by God that are shaping and will continue to shape and shift the political, media, and religious landscape of America in the days ahead.

I know.

I hear you.

These guys? Have you lost your mind, Jeremiah Johnson?

No, my mind is intact! A prophetic dream and encounter on September 15, 2019, convinced me in spite of my personal opinions and beliefs that God has chosen these three men to be wrecking balls to American religious, media, and political beliefs and ideologies.

THE PROPHETIC DREAM

In the dream, I joined thousands of people in an audience as Donald Trump and Kanye West took the stage and shared their faith. It was raw; it was infantile. They said some things that we would hope never to hear at a traditional church service. As they shared, I was intrigued by the audience reaction. Half of the crowd appeared saved but literally manifested demons. They shouted, pointed their fingers, and accused. They refused to accept that these two men were in any way qualified to speak for and about God. They demanded Trump and West demonstrate greater spirituality and articulate spiritual matters with greater sophistication than either are currently capable of.

The other half of the gathered were deeply touched and moved to tears. Their response was stunning.

As tension and division in the room mounted, Justin Bieber strode onto the stage and threw the crowd into utter chaos. Half of the people gathered there cheered Bieber wildly and ecstatically because he had chosen to come out and sing and share about his faith. The other half became so irate they rioted. The toxic atmosphere forced the event to be shut down.

In the midst of this frenzy, I pushed my way to the front to try and get the attention of one of the men on the stage. I found all three in tears, deeply wounded by the response of the rioters and the closure of the meeting. When I had gathered them together, I prophesied to each.

"Kanye," I began, "just as the Lord raised up Donald Trump to be a wrecking ball to this nation, so God has raised you up as another wrecking ball for such a time as this. Trump has wrecked the political landscape in America, but you shall wreck the religious one. You will not say and will not do many things that the Church will expect of you, but heaven has designed events this way. There is a spiritual father you must connect to, a pastor that will take you underneath his wing and protect you from the masses, for this brood of vipers will seek to crucify you ahead your time."

Then I turned to Justin Bieber.

"Justin, how long will you waiver between two opinions?" I admonished him. "How long will you run from Jezebel? For the spirit of Elijah is resting upon you, son, to turn the hearts of fathers back to their sons and the hearts of sons back to their fathers. Out of your own brokenness and pain, there shall be a fresh anointing flowing through you that will heal many. You shall be a wrecking ball to the main stream media as you introduce them to the heart of the Father. Like David, you shall sing and prophesy over a generation the love and mercy of God that endures forever."

Finally I addressed President Trump.

"Donald, says the Lord, I have given you Kanye and Justin as gifts to help bring a greater influence that you will need heading into the 2020 elections. Keep your eyes on Israel and China as I will continue to give you great wisdom that will bring tremendous increase and protection in the days ahead. Like King Josiah, you must not fight battles that are not yours to fight. Allow me to fight the deception taking place in the political arena in America. For I am moving in the media and the Church even now."

And again I woke up.

Upon waking, the Holy Spirit immediately spoke to me from 1 Corinthians: "God has chosen the foolish things of the world to shame the wise, and God has chosen the weak things of the world to shame the things which are strong."

May those who have ears to hear and eyes to see begin praying for Donald Trump, Justin Bieber, and Kanye West with vigor. They each have a significant assignment in the days ahead and the opposition will be fierce, especially among the religious. Each of them will not do and say as other believers will desire, but we must seek to recognize heaven's mandate in this hour. Specifically watch as Kanye West is a secret weapon in the hands of the Lord to win Donald Trump votes from the African American community.

A SECOND PROPHETIC DREAM

The prophetic dream from September 15th concerning Donald Trump, Kanye West, and Justin Bieber went viral around the world. Because of its millions of views, I was invited to do radio and television interviews in many places. I declined, however, believing my assignment as a messenger was complete. In essence, I knew through prayer and fasting that God gave me the prophetic dream so that He might help His people recognize the era we are entering into in the earth.

After two months, to have said that Kanye West is a wrecking ball to the Church is a serious understatement. The "brood of vipers," many of whom are in the Church, have viciously attacked him and questioned his conversion, yet many other Christians have rejoiced and thanked God for his profession of faith in Christ and the platform God has granted him. I personally have been outspoken publicly and privately, warning the Church not to become critical and attack what God is doing with Kanye West.

With that said, I recently received a very troubling prophetic dream concerning Kanye West on November 2nd. I have not felt released to share the dream until now.

In this encounter, Kanye entered a large arena that looked much like a church building. However, the words "Babylon" were written over its doors. A red carpet was rolled out for him and the applause of the people was deafening.

He took the stage and began to sing "Jesus is King." Purity flooded from his heart, but a horrific spirit of idolatry manifested in the church arena. Many in the crowd began to fall down and worship him.

Immediately I recognized this as a battle for his soul. Though his conversion and commitment to the Lord Jesus is pure, an anti-Christ spirit waged war on him in the dream. To my shock, the anti-Christ spirit was emerging from within the church.

In my dream, I ran to the stage and urged Kanye to get off of it. Leaning down so he could hear me in spite of the crowd's roar, I prophesied to him: "Those who love entertainment and the false gospel of prosperity seek to devour the pure anointing upon your life even now. Jezebel has come for your vineyard and you must refuse to give it up. Do not open the garden of your heart to those who will try to entice and make deals and alliances with you. Kanye, you must avoid the unholy alliances and the idolatry of the people in the coming season. Beware!"

I woke up from this prophetic dream in deep intercession and travail. As I began to cry out under the intense burden of the Lord, my prayers reached out toward the millions of Christians around the world who are now supporting and watching Kanye as never before. If by chance you heard and/or read the first prophetic dream God gave me in September, I now warn the body of Christ that Kanye West is in grave danger of being polluted by a spirit of anti-Christ from within the church. This spirit desires to draw the worship of Jesus Christ to worship of Kanye West and seduce him into believing a false gospel of prosperity and entertainment. A Babylonian spirit runs rampant in parts of the church and this spirit has been assigned to take Kanye out and silence the prophetic voice God has given him for our generation.

Would you please join me right now in covering Kanye West and his family in prayer and intercession? Target this spirit of anti-Christ that is warring against his soul, trying to seduce him with the love of money, fame, and applause. The Babylonian spirit of entertainment and prosperity will try to allure him into compromising the pure prophetic anointing God has given him.

May we be quick to recognize that God has called Kanye West for such a time as this, but may we also be quick to understand and pray against the propensity of so many, especially in the church, to elevate him to a height that God never intended to give him.

Only Jesus is worthy of being the center of our adoration and praise.

CHAPTER 7   Prayer Points

For President Trump:
- Pray that God would raise up spiritual fathers to advise and protect him.
- Pray that he would see Israel and China with spiritual eyes.
- Pray that God gives him a spirit of wisdom and revelation in the knowledge of Jesus.
- Pray that President Trump allows the Lord to fight for him.
- Pray Exodus 14:14.

For Kanye West:
- Pray that God protects him from pride and deception.
- Ask the Lord to cut off flattering lips and deliver him from the snare of the trapper.
- Pray Psalm 12:3 and Psalm 91:3.

For Justin Bieber:
- Pray that God would anoint him with spiritual songs that restore relationships, heal hearts, and shine forth the love of God.

For all three:
- Pray the Lord's protection over them.
- Pray for the Lord's grace and wisdom to rest on them.
- Pray that God would be their strong tower.
- Pray God will open the eyes of the Church to stop judging each other and to walk in love.
- Pray Romans 14:10, Matthew 7:1, and Ephesians 5:2.

CHAPTER 8

WILL THE SWAMP DRAIN TRUMP?

I have been a nightly dreamer since the days of my youth, but I cannot remember the last time I had a nightmare. That all changed dramatically in early January of 2019. I woke up in my bed unable to breathe, my heart racing out of control, and my entire body numb and shaking. It was a terrifying experience.

In the dream, I was on a ship with Donald Trump in a swamp infested with alligators. Many of these creatures were more than twenty feet long. However, they were not merely alligators; in the dream they revealed themselves to me as "mercenary alligators." In other words, they were trained to sink our ship and had no other agenda. They did not hesitate to risk their lives to accomplish their mission. They had been commissioned to sink the ship and kill us.

As our ship sailed deeper into the swamp, Donald Trump was laughing, wearing his "Make America Great Again" hat as he steered. He continued to laugh, purposely plowing into as many alligators as he could.

"I'm going to drain this swamp!" he would yell to me across the ship.

Suddenly, I realized that the more Trump tried to drain the swamp, the more the swamp was draining him. Larger and larger alligators surfaced. They swam to our ship and bit large chunks out of it. The ship began to take on water. I knew that death was imminent, but the President appeared totally oblivious to the great danger we were in.

I pleaded with him to stop intentionally and purposely draining the swamp but it was too late. We were swallowed by a mercenary alligator and found ourselves in a gigantic black hole—a mercenary alligator abyss. I heard hordes of demons laughing and cheering. What I felt and experienced as Donald Trump and I died together is something I can never forget.

I awoke in my bed, suffocating, numb, with a heart racing out of my chest. I prayed to God to set me free, and this is how the Lord answered me:

> "Jeremiah, My people do not recognize the demonic warfare from hell that is being unleashed upon the United States and Donald Trump. Even as a wall is being built, why are My people refusing to build a wall of intercession and prayer around their President and around their nation? Yes, the borders are unsecured but they are far more unsecured in the spirit realm than you could possibly imagine. How is it that a man would see the necessity of

building a wall to protect a country but My people cannot even recognize their desperate need to build a wall of intercession and prayer around their own lives and churches? How the American Church continues to sleep and slumber in these days of history has come before My throne and greatly grieved My heart!"

He continued:

"I warn you, Jeremiah, that as Donald Trump tries to drain the Swamp, the Swamp is going to drain him. His heart will become hardened, his resolve will become dangerous, and the attacks upon his life and presidency will get bigger and bigger. These things will largely come to pass because of a prayerless Church in America, a Church that refuses to pray for their President and ignores the demonic agendas in Washington. If My people do not begin to gather and call upon My name, great danger will come upon the shores of the United States of America."

DONALD TRUMP AND POLITICAL WARFARE

On November 15, 2019, I had another alarming dream in which Washington D.C. had turned into a huge jungle absolutely infested with snakes.

I found Donald Trump and his wife Melanie forced down into a bunker of some sorts. I somehow knew exactly where to find them. They told me they were forced to go underground because they could no longer discern between true friends and enemies. I tried to encourage the President that the Church was praying for them but it was of no avail. He was too emotionally and physically exhausted to listen.

The President then told me of a specific command post in Washington D.C. where I could survey the land and then come back and give him a report.

I went out into the jungle and climbed an ancient and very tall, thick tree.

When I reached the top, I started shouting over the nation's capital, "Guerrilla warfare! Yes, and I tell you more! It's called, 'Political Warfare' and it's as real as the devil is real. Can anyone hear me?!"

I returned to Donald Trump and reported what I had seen and heard. I told him Washington D.C. had been overrun by guerrilla and political warfare and his life was in great danger. With tears in his eyes, he said, "I thought you said the Church has been praying for me."

Then I awoke.

Those who desire to respond to this prophetic dream in an appropriate manner should read the following carefully.

EXPOSING GUERRILLA WARFARE

The main strategy and tactics of guerrilla warfare involve the use of a small attacking, mobile force against a large, unwieldy force. The guerrilla force is largely or entirely organized in small units that are dependent on the support of the local population. Tactically, the guerrilla army makes the repetitive attacks far from the opponent's center of gravity with a view to keeping its own casualties to a minimum and imposing a constant debilitating strain on the enemy. This may provoke the enemy into a brutal, excessively destructive response which will anger and alienate their support base while increasing support for the guerrillas, ultimately compelling the enemy to relinquish territory.

THE STRATEGY OF THE DEVIL

While I agree that Donald Trump has been chosen by God to address many issues in the United States, I also believe that the devil wants to wear him down and draw him into battles that are not his to fight. Both the alligator dream and the guerrilla warfare dream speak to the necessity of the Church to engage in strategic intercession concerning the plans of the enemy. Remember that the tactics of guerrilla warfare are intended to provoke a destructive and overly angry response from its victim. The "Swamp" in Washington D.C. is maneuvering Donald Trump into an angry and reactionary state. Their strategy is to provoke him into a costly mistake that will give them grounds to accuse and impeach him.

Are you praying for your president?

CHAPTER 8   Prayer Points

- Sound the alarm! Call for the Church to rise up; ask God to again awaken the Church.
- Pray Ephesians 5:14-17.
- Pray for the Spirit of Prayer to touch hearts.
- Ask for divine protection for President Trump.
- Declare Isaiah 54:17 over President Trump.
- Pray that President Trump will not grow weary in well doing and will not lose heart (Galatians 6:9).
- Pray for God to keep the President from stumbling and to make him stand in the presence of His glory blameless with great joy (Jude 1:24).
- Call for truth, light, and righteousness to be released over our nation.
- Pray for the heart of our nation to be turned back to God.

CHAPTER 9

THE WINNER OF
THE 2020 ELECTION

The most frequent question I receive from leaders and saints all over the world is this: Will Donald Trump win the 2020 election?

One well-known Christian leader recently boasted to me that "Donald Trump has the 2020 election in the bag; we don't even need to pray and worry about it. We can just sit back and watch him drain the swamp with ease."

Because of the revelation the Lord has given me, imagine how deeply my heart was grieved and alarmed by this remark.

THE BOSTON MARATHON

On a long fast seeking the Lord about the 2020 elections, I was given a prophetic dream that allows me to answer the above question in part.

In the dream, Donald Trump was running the Boston Marathon. The crowds gathered along the path of the race were not there to support him but to mock and jeer at him. Many spat at him, and without security present, I am convinced they would have physically harmed him. As the President drew within one hundred yards of the finish line, he stumbled and fell.

Completely exhausted and having heart issues, he could not get up from the ground.

The crowd went wild; their applause was ear-piercing. I watched with mounting sorrow and despair, but suddenly hope filled my heart.

Out of the crowd, two older women, one with a cane and one with a walker, somehow slipped through security and came to the President's aid. From a physical standpoint, I thought to myself in the dream, "How could these two old ladies with their cane and walker even pick up an exhausted Donald Trump, let alone take him to the finish line?"

In the natural, it was impossible. But as I looked closely, something like a rushing wind fell upon these two old women and they supernaturally picked the President off the ground and helped him across the finish line. Mike Pence, Franklin Graham, Donald Trump Jr, and his family were there to comfort him. He had finished the race, but he could not have done so without the supernatural intervention of two old women.

THE INTERPRETATION

I believe Donald Trump will win the 2020 election, but he cannot do it without supernatural intervention. The two old women represented the role of the praying Church in 2020. Without their activism and aid, I am deeply afraid the attacks and warfare launched from the liberal base will prove too much for him to overcome.

For Donald Trump to win the 2020 election, the Baby Boomers must arise in America and take a stand. The future of America belongs to this generation in this season. I see many Baby Boomers who are currently in full time ministry shifting out of their roles to get heavily involved in politics in 2020. Many pastors will feel a tremendous burden from God to mobilize their congregations with days of prayer and fasting for Trump and the future of America.

Expect attacks against President Trump to arise in Boston (representing the liberal media and agenda) with greater ferocity than ever before. If they cannot impeach him, they will attempt assassination. I, for one, pray that our President's fate will not reflect the fate of Abraham Lincoln.

A CHURCH THAT MUST BE UNITED

If Christians across America are realistic about the true nature of the faith of our founding fathers, they will stop demanding of Donald Trump a religious standard that he cannot meet.

Yes, Donald Trump is an immature Christian, but he is also pro-life. He has taken a politically unpopular and even courageous stand against the shedding of innocent blood in the United States. The Church must refuse to vote for any political candidate regardless of political party who supports abortion.

We must keep our eyes open to the revival that is coming to the media mountain. God is raising up Kanye West as another wrecking ball that will help bring in a mighty harvest of souls to this nation.

Finally, I firmly believe that the future of America in this season is in the hands of the Baby Boomers. If they will support Donald Trump and raise their voice against the national shedding of innocent blood, I believe Trump will win re-election in 2020.

If the Baby Boomers do not rise and become prophetic activists, I do not believe President Trump will make it to the finish line. The attacks and warfare waged against him will be too much, affecting even his physical body.

As 2020 begins, meditate on the following words of Abraham Kuyper, Prime Minister of the Netherlands in the early 1900s: "When principles that run against your deepest convictions begin to win the day, then battle is your calling, and peace has become sin; you must, at the price of dearest peace, lay your convictions bare before friend and enemy, with all the fire of your faith."

May the praying Church enter into battle; may we refuse to be silent any longer. Let us lay our convictions bare before friends and enemies alike and ask God to bless America once again!

CHAPTER 9   Prayer Points

- Pray for a prayer movement—for a chorus of prayer to be released over our nation.
- Pray for our Baby Boomers to arise and be encouraged and to pray for our elections.
- Pray for our spiritual leaders to have courage to speak about elections, abortion, and racism in the pulpits.

CHAPTER 10

THE FUTURE OF AMERICA BELONGS TO THE BABY BOOMERS

Baby Boomers, born in the post-World-War-2 years of 1945 to 1964, are currently fifty-five to seventy-five years old. They represent almost one-fourth of the total population of the United States of America—approximately 76 million people.[36] They are called Baby Boomers because of their huge numbers, swelling the nurseries of Americas in the wake of returning GIs after World War 2.

For a generation known as "baby boomers," consider the irony that, in the days of their youth (1973), *Roe v. Wade* was decided by the Supreme Court, initiating the murder of millions of babies. Put another way, perhaps *Roe v. Wade* was a direct attack on the prophetic destiny of a baby boomer generation called to stand for life in an America seduced by materialism. Interestingly, that's exactly the strategy the

---

36. U.S. Department of Commerce, Economics and Statistics Administration, U.S. Census Bureau, *The Baby Boom Cohort in the United States: 2012–2060: Population Estimates and Projections*, by Sandra L. Colby and Jennifer M. Ortman, May 2014, P25-1141, https://www.census.gov/prod/2014pubs/p25-1141.pdf.

devil tried when Moses was born and when Jesus was born. Pharoah killed all the children of Moses' generation at birth or infancy, and Herod killed the children two years and younger in Bethlehem in Jesus' generation.

Heading into the 2020 election, God has spoken to me that the future of America now rests in the hands of the Baby Boomers. How will this generation of Christian saints and leaders respond to the challenges of the present moment in American history?

I believe God wants to encourage this generation that they have been prepared for this moment like Esther. Now is the time for Baby Boomers to lift their voices together against abortion and for the re-election of Donald Trump!

Why?

Because the lives of their children and grandchildren depend on it.

A special anointing rests upon this generation to move the United States into the fullness of her God-given destiny. Should Baby Boomers fail to respond to this call, the cost exacted from them will be the lives of their children and grandchildren.

It would be a terrible price to pay.

HERE COME THE BABY BOOMERS

God has shown me that many men and women in the body of Christ born between 1946 and 1964 have been "overlooked." In the years ahead, God will begin promoting and favoring these men and women in the body of Christ and reward them for their faithfulness and courage even when they have suffered multiple disappointments and great rejection.

I heard the Lord say, "Great wisdom is missing in My body."

"Where is it, Lord?" I asked.

"It is with the Baby Boomers who have been over-looked," He replied, "but now they will be revealed and carry great wisdom to My body for such a time as this!"

If you were born between 1946 and 1964, God is saying to you, "These are the best years of your life! Refuse to feel sorry for yourself! Refuse to believe that I have left you on the sidelines! I say to you this year, it is time to get off the bench and get in the game. The young generations are in great need of the wisdom you carry, wisdom that has been purchased at great cost from your own failures and mistakes. You have much to offer and if you are willing and available, I will cause a vibrancy and fresh wind of My Spirit to come upon you and enable you to fulfill My will in and around you."

"Some of you have even had some measures of success in your younger years," says your God, "but have fallen prey to discouragement over the last ten years. I will strengthen you; I will cause you to rise to the occasion and fulfill the assignments I am about to release to you this year. Be encouraged and of good cheer. I will fight for you and win your heart over to me like never before."

"This is your year!" says God. "Books are still to be written, young people are still to be led to Jesus. Projects must be completed. Some of you will even marry. You will not be defined by your divorce. Do not become discouraged! I, the Lord your God, am with you and for you!"

A PRAYER OF BLESSING FROM A SON

As a son and millennial in the body of Christ whose parents are Baby Boomers, I want to lift my voice and bless you! To those Baby Boomers and grandparents who have read this book and have children my age who have fallen away from the Lord, do not let the devil shame and guilt trip you for another day. In 2020 and the years ahead, many relationships shall be radically restored and reconciled across America. The spirit and power of Elijah that turns the hearts of fathers and sons back towards one another will overtake many. I honor, bless, and repent of the pain and hurt caused by the rebellion of your children.

I say to you, "Rise up! Fight! Know that a new era is dawning!"

The future of America belongs to you!

CHAPTER 10   Prayer Points

- Pray for an anointing of wisdom upon the older generation.
- Pray for a fresh wind of the Spirit to come upon the Baby Boomers.
- Pray that God would mend the hearts of the Baby Boomers.
- Pray for the Baby Boomers to seek wisdom and strength.
- Pray for the Baby Boomers to be restored and to be healed.
- Pray the full armor of God over the Baby Boomers.
- Pray that the Baby Boomers would rise up again, take their place in the front lines of the army of God, and go to war!
- Pray for God's anointing to be upon this book so that all who read it will be stirred to rise up and pray for our President and our nation.

AFTERWORD

The only thing standing between America and the swift and terrible judgment of the Lord is His Bride. Do you doubt that we are ripe for judgment? Have you grown so comfortable with the evil around you that you are no longer stirred to travail in prayer and fasting to abate the well-deserved judgment of our Consuming Fire God? If so, let me provide you with some motivation. Three thousand babies are executed every day in America by a paid assassin. Who is paying the assassins? The babies' very own parents!

SODOMITES AND DRAG QUEENS

Sodomite parades are attended by hundreds of thousands of citizens every year in America. These lewd parades, which celebrate all manner of sexual anarchy, are attended by small children and welcomed by elected city officials.

Taxpayer-funded public schools in almost every school district in America are teaching little boys that they might actually be girls, and vice versa, resulting in thousands of young people per year permanently mutilating their bodies through sex reassignment surgeries. Children are being allowed to dance in provocative drag queen performances inside of homosexual bars while grown homosexual men throw money at them for their performances. Though reported to local authorities, no actions are taken to stop this pedophilic behavior. No one wants to anger the LGBT community, so children go entirely unprotected and continue to be violated and exploited. We have become monsters. Absolute monsters and savages. Nations that were seemingly undefeatable have been humiliated and decimated by our God when they embraced the evils of child sacrifice and sexual anarchy as we have.

In Noah's day, God was so grieved He made man that He wiped out the world population with a devastating flood of judgment. In AD 70, after the Jews rejected the Messiah and violently crucified Him to a cross, the Romans besieged them until the Jews were eating their own children. So many Jews were crucified on crucifixes (500 per day) that there were no trees to be found in the area. If this type of judgment could devastate the apple of God's eye, what type of judgment are we due? Six of the seven churches mentioned in Revelation 2 and 3 were destroyed by Muslim hordes after God warned them He would remove their candlestick.

Do we really think we are immune to God's punishment as a nation after openly spurning His law and celebrating sin? God warned His people in Deuteronomy 28:62-63, "You who were as numerous as the stars in the sky will be left but few in number, because you did not obey the LORD your God. Just as it pleased the LORD to make you prosper and increase in number, so it will please him to ruin and destroy you. You will be uprooted from the land you are entering to possess."

Surely the blood of 60 million aborted babies cries out to God for judgment. How has God not already destroyed us? The answer can be found in Genesis 18, where God tells Abraham if He can find a mere 10 righteous people in the evil city of Sodom, He will spare the entire city His judgment. God is certainly not obligated to have mercy on us, but I believe the faithful service and intercession of God's people is currently abating His full wrath. What a powerful thought to ponder that we can stand in the gap for our nation through fasting and prayer and partner with God to usher in spiritual revival.

OUR HOPE IS IN GOD

In America, we tend to place a great emphasis on presidential policies, but be encouraged, church of the living God, President Trump is not the answer, God is! And He chooses to allow us to partner with Him through intercession. Jesus didn't tell us "the gates of hell will not prevail against the Republican Party." He said, "The gates of hell will not prevail against My church." America's intercessors and wall watchmen are holding back the wrath of God. We are the thin veil of beautiful incense that wafts up to the heavenlies as a reminder to a holy God that the sacrifice of His Son has not been in vain.

To interpose means to insert oneself between one thing and another. God has given us beautiful and inspiring examples in Scripture of the power of believers to interpose on behalf of a nation or people group. I can't read these examples without a fresh anointing of intercessory inspiration. Let's take a quick peek and ask God to burden us afresh to stand in the gap for our nation.

When God was fed up with Israel's sin and about to crush them like a gnat, Moses stepped in between them and pleaded with God to reconsider, and God did. Did you hear that? A man stepped in between the God of the universe and his ungrateful, petulant, hard-hearted children and won God's mercy for them.

Moses' God is the very same God we serve today. Are we behaving as if we have the ability to alter history? Are we praying and fasting and laboring as if we could influence God with regard to national judgment? What if Moses had chosen food and popularity over fasting and travailing and waiting on God? How different might the Hebrew story be?

WE MUST RISE

When the Jewish people were about to be destroyed by Haman's unrighteous law, Esther risked her life and leveraged her influence and position to stand in the gap between a people group and an unrighteousness law. Laws were changed and an entire people group saved because Esther listened to wise counsel, fasted and prayed, risked her position, and spoke the truth boldly. What if Esther had chosen the safety of silence and the comfort of her position over the risk of interposition? Thankfully, Esther said yes to God and a seemingly impossible victory was won.

Do you want God to use you that way? Do you want unrighteous laws to be changed in our nation? Do you want the 3,000 precious babies who are executed every day in America to be rescued and protected by law? This kind of cultural revival won't happen until the Lord's Bride loves the smile of God more than the favor of man.

Everyone wants to do great things like Moses and Esther did, but who is willing to carry the cross they carried? Who is willing to risk their lives to stand in the gap for others? Who is willing to leverage their place of power and influence to confront the idolatry and corruption of their day? "For the eyes of the LORD run to and fro throughout the whole earth, to show himself strong in the behalf of them whose heart is perfect toward him." (2 Chronicles 16:9)

A CALL TO ACTION

In this book, Jeremiah Johnson has given us a serious call to intercessory prayer for our President and our nation. I want to reinforce that admonition with a very hearty "Amen" and an exhortation to put more faithful and frequent ACTION to our prayers. What would Jesus' travailing prayer in the Garden of Gethsemane have accomplished if He hadn't rolled up his sleeves and died on a cruel cross for you and me? What would Esther's prayers have accomplished if she hadn't risked her life, scheduled a meeting, cooked a meal and outed Haman?

Some of you need to be the answer to America's abortion crisis by ministering on the sidewalks of America's abortion centers or by running for Governor and trusting God to help you end the bloodshed in your state. Some of you need to protect vulnerable children in your community by mobilizing parents and grandparents to your City Council meetings to push out the dangerous transgender bathroom agenda.

Some of you need to be the answer to the pornographic sex ed crisis in your community by running for your local school board to fight obscenity in the schools and school libraries. If not you, then who? Has not God called us to be salt and light in the world?

I believe America was planted by the miraculous power of God in order to bless every corner of the earth with the light of the Gospel and to push back the darkness of communism, atheism and Islam. There is an all-out war to make sure America is sucked into the same black hole of darkness that much of the world is experiencing as we speak.

Have you ever noticed how the forces of darkness are never satisfied unless they gain more ground, unless more babies are killed, unless more children are sexualized? The workers of iniquity seem to have an abundance of energy and resources to promote evil, do they not? It's nothing short of demonic.

GET TO WORK

In contrast, have you ever noticed the strange amount of lethargy and complacency that plagues the church when it comes to fasting and praying and fighting evil in our culture? It is likewise demonic. We are so satisfied with things as they are. And yet, the wicked continue to use their energy to gain new ground.

What has God laid on your heart to do for Him? Have you been obedient? Rise up and shake off fear and doubt. Do we not have the God of Heaven and all His hosts on our side to aid us? We must tap into His strength and power if we are going to partner with Christ to build His kingdom on Earth as it is in Heaven.

There is a growing prophetic movement that loves to receive a WORD from God, but they don't want to WORK for God. God doesn't need professional churchgoers or conference attendees. Salt serves no purpose if it's only sitting in the shaker. His Kingdom is for the sharing. Jesus didn't tell us to hide and hunker down until He returns. He said, "Occupy until I return." There is work to do. There is a Kingdom to build. Let's build it for the glory of God!

—Elizabeth Johnston, homeschooling mother of ten children, speaker, bestselling author of *Not On My Watch* and creator of the *Activist Mommy*. To follow, please visit www.ActivistMommy.com

Day Of Mourning, Organizer
www.DayOfMourning.org

Sex Ed Sit Out, Organizer
www.SexEdSitOut.com

Order my bestselling book "Not On My Watch"
https://activistmommy.com/book/